Winnie Makes Trouble

LAURA OWEN & KORKY PAUL

OXFORD
UNIVERSITY PRESS

Helping your child to read

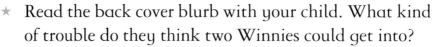
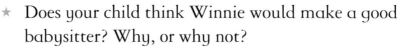

Before they start

- ★ Read the back cover blurb with your child. What kind of trouble do they think two Winnies could get into?
- ★ Does your child think Winnie would make a good babysitter? Why, or why not?

During reading

- ★ Let your child read at their own pace – don't worry if it's slow. Offer them plenty of help if they get stuck, and enjoy the story together.
- ★ Help them to work out words they don't know by saying each sound out loud and then blending them to say the word, e.g. *p-ar-s-n-i-p-s, parsnips*.
- ★ If your child still struggles with a word, just tell them the word and move on.
- ★ Give them lots of praise for good reading!

After reading

- ★ Look at page 48 for some fun activities.

Contents

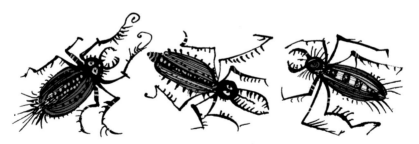

OXFORD
UNIVERSITY PRESS

Great Clarendon Street, Oxford OX2 6DP
Oxford University Press is a department of the University of Oxford.
It furthers the University's objective of excellence in research, scholarship,
and education by publishing worldwide. Oxford is a registered trade mark
of Oxford University Press in the UK and in certain other countries

"Winnie's Double" was first published in *Winnie Spells Trouble* 2014
"Winnie Minds the Baby" was first published in *Winnie Goes for Gold* 2012

This edition published 2020

British Library Cataloguing in Publication Data

Data available

ISBN: 978-0-19-277373-9

1 3 5 7 9 10 8 6 4 2

Printed in China

Paper used in the production of this book is a natural,
recyclable product made from wood grown in sustainable forests.
The manufacturing process conforms to the environmental
regulations of the country of origin.

Acknowledgements
With thanks to Caterine Baker for editorial support.

Winnie's Double

Winnie was trying to get dressed. The trouble was,

she had lost one of her long socks!

"Drat and double drat, Wilbur!" said Winnie. "Where has that sock gone?"

But Wilbur didn't know. "Meeow?" he said, handing Winnie her wand.

"Good idea, Wilbur!" said Winnie. "I'll do a doubling spell, and magic up another sock!"

So Winnie stood in front of her mirror. She waved her magic wand once . . . twice . . . "**Abracadabra!**"

Suddenly, there were *two* Winnies!

"Who in the witchy world are you?" asked Winnie, staring at the other Winnie.

"I'm Winnie!" said the other Winnie.

"Me, too!" said the first Winnie.

"Don't you mean 'me two'?" laughed the other

Winnie. "We're witchy twins!"

Both Winnies started dancing around in circles.

Soon Wilbur couldn't tell which witch was which!

"Meeow!" said Wilbur.

"Wilbur's hungry!" said the Winnies.

So they *both* fetched Wilbur some breakfast.

"**Purrr!**" Wilbur tucked into a big bowl of zingy stringy treats.

"Oh, Wilbur!" moaned one Winnie. "Don't you like my floppy fish?"

She looked so sad that Wilbur started to eat the fish instead.

But then the *other* Winnie started moaning!

So Wilbur tried hard to eat both breakfasts.

He didn't want to upset either of the Winnies.

But which was the real Winnie – his Winnie?

He just couldn't tell.

The two Winnies seemed quite happy, though.

Just then, the doorbell rang.

Brriiiinnnggg!
Wiiiinnnniiiieeee!

"Who can that be?" said both Winnies.

Both Winnies ran to open the door. It was the post lady.

"I have a parcel for Winnie the Witch," she said.

"That's me!" said both Winnies.

Both Winnies grabbed the parcel. They pulled off the paper, and inside was a shiny new broom.

"Mine!" shouted both Winnies, and they both jumped on.

But the two Winnies were too heavy for the broom. It began to **wobble** and **wibble**.

"Get off! This is my broom!" said one Winnie.

"No, *you* get off!"

said the other Winnie.

The broom took off,

with a **wobble** and

a **wibble**.

It flew slowly out

into the garden . . .

. . . and tipped both Winnies into the pond!

Splosh! Splash!

Now the Winnies were wet, and slimy, and cross with each other.

"I'm going to magic you away!" said one Winnie.

"No, *I'm* going to magic *you* away!" said the other.

But both Winnies had lost their wands in the pond! Wilbur ran back inside and found a spare wand.

But which Winnie should he give it to? Which was the *real* Winnie?

"I'm the real Winnie!" said one of them. "You must recognise me, Wilbur!"

"No, it's me, Wilbur!" said the other one. "Don't listen to her!"

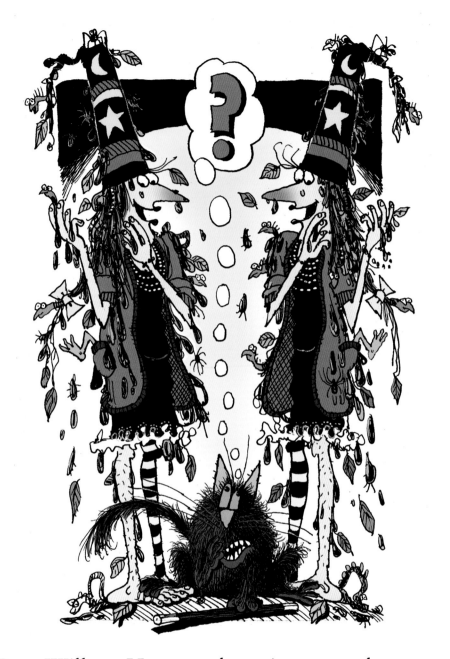

Poor Wilbur. How was he going to work out which was the right Winnie?

Just then, Wilbur spotted something.

One Winnie had a sock on her right leg, and one Winnie had a sock on her left leg.

Wilbur thought hard. That morning, his Winnie had had a sock on her right leg.

So Wilbur gave the wand to that Winnie.

"Thank you, clever old Wilbur!" said the
real Winnie.

She waved the wand, and shouted,

"Abracadabra!"

At once, the other Winnie vanished.

"Well, thank slimy slugs she's gone!" said Winnie.

"Meeow!" said Wilbur, happily.

Winnie looked at her bare left leg.

"I don't need another sock, Wilbur," she said.

"Why should both legs be the same? I've gone off things that are the same as each other."

"Meeow!" agreed Wilbur.

Winnie Minds the Baby

"What shall we do today, Wilbur?" said Winnie, one beautiful sunny day. "I fancy going to the park!"

"Meeeow!" said Wilbur happily.

Suddenly, they heard a *very* loud noise.

Weeeaaaaah! Weeeaaaaah!

Wilbur put his paws over his ears.

"That sounds just like you did when I trod on your tail, Wilbur," said Winnie. "Whatever can it be?"

WEEEAAAAAH!

went the noise again.

"Pickled parsnips, it's getting worse!" said Winnie.

Just then, they saw a lady pushing a pram around the corner.

"I think your pram wheels need oiling," said Winnie to the lady.

"It's not the wheels, Winnie," said the lady.

"It's my baby. He won't stop crying!"

Winnie looked down at the baby. "**Coochie-coochie-coo!**" she said.

The baby started laughing.

"Wow, Winnie!" said the baby's mum. "You've made him laugh! You're wonderful with babies!"

"**Goo-goo!**" said the baby.

"**Yaaawn!**" went the lady.

Suddenly, Winnie had a good idea. "Why don't you have a nap in my hammock? Wilbur and I can look after the baby."

Wilbur wasn't sure. "Meeow?"

"Oh, thank you!" said the baby's mum. She jumped into the hammock. Soon she was fast asleep.

"Ssssh!" Winnie whispered to Wilbur and the baby. "Come on. Let's go to the park!"

So off they went.

At first, everything went well.

It was fun on the swings.

"**Goo!**" said the baby.

"**wheeee!**" said Winnie, swinging as high as she could.

But just then . . .

Winnie's shoe flew off.

whoosh!

It landed with a **plop** in someone's picnic.

"Goo-goo-goo!" laughed the baby.

"Let's try the see-saw next!" said Winnie.

Winnie sat down hard on one end – and Wilbur whizzed up into the air.

"**Goo-goo-goo-goo-goo!**" laughed the baby.

But then the baby yelled.

"**weeeaaaaah!**"

"Oh no!" said Winnie. "What's wrong, baby?"

"**weeeeaaaaaaah!**"

Wilbur pointed at the baby's nappy.

"Pooh!" said Winnie. "He needs a new nappy."

She tried to make a nappy out of moss and leaves.

It was a bit scratchy, though. The baby started

wriggling and pulling Winnie's nose.

"Oh, nattering newts!" said Winnie. "You need a nap! I'll sing you a sleepytime song:

"Close your eyes now, little boy!
Don't be weepy, just be sleepy,
Close your eyes now, little boy!"

"**weeeeaaaaah!**" yelled the baby.

"Oh, drat and double drat!" said Winnie.

"**Abracadabra!**"

And she magicked up some dancing ducks and squirrels to make the baby happy.

That didn't work either.

"weeeeeeeaaaaaaaaah!"

"I wish this baby was more like a grown-up!" sighed Winnie. "Why can't he walk and talk?"

That gave her another good idea.

"Abracadabra!"

The baby looked at Winnie. "Good afternoon!" he said. Then he started running down the path. "Greetings, fellow animals!" he called. But the duck and the squirrel hurried away fast. **Whooosh!**

"Catch him, Wilbur!" said Winnie.

They caught him just as he got back to
Winnie's gate.

"**Abracadabra!**" said Winnie. The baby
changed back to his normal self just before his
mother arrived!

"Hello, darling!" said the baby's mum. "Have you been a good boy for Winnie?"

"Gurgle-wurgle-goo!" said the baby.

"Thank you, Winnie!" said the baby's mum. "How amazing! You've taught him to talk!"

And they went home together happily.

"I'm worn out!" said Winnie. "Babies are such hard work. I'll stick to cats from now on!"

"Meeow!" agreed Wilbur happily.

After reading activities

Talk about the stories

Ask your child the following questions. Encourage them to talk about their answers.

1) In "Winnie's Double", what is in the package that arrived for the two Winnies?

2) In "Winnie's Double", how do you think Winnie and Wilbur feel at the end of the story?

3) In "Winnie Minds the Baby", does Winnie change her mind about babies? Why?

1) A broomstick; 2) Probably relieved that everything is back to normal; 3) At first she thinks babies are easy to look after. Later she realises they are a lot of hard work.

Try this!

Make up a spell for Winnie. Draw what happens when she uses your special spell!